JIM PIPE

WITCHES

COPPER BEECH BOOKS
BROOKFIELD, CONNECTICUT

© Aladdin Books Ltd 1997
© U.S. text 1997

Designed and produced by
Aladdin Books Ltd
28 Percy Street
London W1P OLD

First published in
the United States in 1997 by
Copper Beech Books
an imprint of The Millbrook Press
2 Old New Milford Road
Brookfield, Connecticut 06804

Editor
Jon Richards
Design
David West Children's Book Design
Designer
Flick Killerby
Picture Research
Brooks Krikler Research
Illustrator
Richard Rockwood
Using Photography By
Roger Vlitos

Printed in Belgium

Library of Congress Cataloging-in-Publication Data
Pipe, Jim, 1966-
Witches / Jim Pipe ; illustrated by Richard Rockwood.
p. cm.
Includes index.
Summary: An account of the powers, spells, and potions of
witches in ancient and medieval times as well as in America ;
includes warlocks, magicians, witchdoctors, and sorcerers.
ISBN 0-7613-0607-2 (lib. bdg.)
1. Witches—Juvenile literature. [1. Witches.]
I. Rockwood, Richard, ill. II. Title.
BF1566.P57 1997   97-75460
133.4'3—dc21   CIP AC

CONTENTS

WITCHES
• They'll put a spell on you •

Rachel was bored. It was so unfair to be stuck in a stuffy old classroom listening to Mr. Raven drone on about atoms when it was so beautiful outside. Then Nathan whispered, "Hey, have you heard about the strange old woman who's moved into number 69? Do you think she's a witch?" "That's not very nice," said Rachel. "Anyway, her name is Miss Proctor and she only looks strange because everyone else around here is so boring."

Then Rachel jumped as Mr. Raven's voice boomed behind her. "If you've got something to say, perhaps you'd like to share it with the rest of us." Mr. Raven was so creepy – he had this amazing ability to appear from nowhere. "Uh...Nathan told me that Miss Proctor's a witch." Rachel blushed as she spoke – how did Mr. Raven always get you to say the truth? "You foolish girl," he scolded. "You should know better than to believe in such nonsense."

$$X + Y \, 925 \quad 17\frac{3}{3} = X + Z \, \frac{9}{2^4}$$

$$H_0^2 \, 9 \times 10^{41}$$

$$Z^4 \, 297 + \frac{z}{y}^5 = \frac{X+Y}{17^5}$$

$$Z \times \frac{8}{2 \times y} = \frac{2 \, 2^2 + X^y}{2 - X}$$

THE WORLD OF WITCHES

Come, step into the magical realm of spells, potions, and charms, where nothing is quite what it seems. Leave behind the world of science, of what is and is not, and let your imagination run free. This is the world of witches, a world of souls trapped in animal bodies, of strange happenings and enchanted forests. Here, anything is possible...

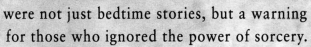

MAGIC POWERS

Most cultures have a tradition of good and bad magic, of terrifying spells and sorcerers using such supernatural powers as:

- ✹ seeing into the future (*right*);
- ✹ flying, raising storms, or becoming invisible;
- ✹ changing themselves or others into animals.

Today, not many people really believe in witches, but not so long ago, magic was taken very seriously. Tales, like that of the Russian witch Baba Yaga (*above left*), were not just bedtime stories, but a warning for those who ignored the power of sorcery.

DO THEY OR DON'T THEY?

What is a witch, and do they really exist? For centuries, people have been accused of causing sickness, bad luck, and even death using evil magic. In 16th-century Europe, thousands were persecuted and killed for witchcraft. But did they really fly on broomsticks or conjure up evil spirits? Perhaps they were just creating healing potions for their friends, or were clever illusionists like the magicians of today (*left*).

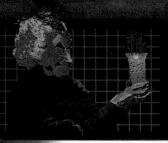

Later, as she wandered home with Emily, her twin, Rachel apologized to Nathan. "It's cool," he said. "Anyway, ignore Mr. Raven. I think we should go and investigate Miss Proctor for ourselves."

"Do you think we should?" replied Rachel. "Mom told us to leave her alone." Emily sneered, "Oh, you're such a goody-goody Rachel. Come on Nathan, let's check out mad Miss P." Rachel wasn't going to let Emily get the better of her. "OK, I'm coming. But we'd better hurry up if we're going to get home before dark." "Scaredy-cat, scaredy-cat," cried Emily, skipping away.

By the time the three children reached Miss Proctor's house on the edge of town, it was already getting dark. Even Emily was nervous, and she jumped when a cat shot out from behind a bush. "Sshh," whispered Nathan.

They tiptoed up to the window. There was Miss Proctor and two friends cooking together. "I told you..." said Rachel, but before she could finish, Nathan gasped, "Yuk — just take a look at those ingredients..."

ANCIENT MAGIC

Early humans viewed the world around them with a mixture of awe and terror. They blamed supernatural forces for powerful events like storms and plagues. Some people even claimed to have direct control over these supernatural forces.

STAR SIGNS

Four thousand years ago, the Egyptians believed that magical powers influenced the world. They created the zodiac (*above*) to explain how the stars and planets guided events on earth – many people still read their horoscope today.

BRING ME YOUR PUPPIES!

The Egyptian belief in magic spread to ancient Greece. In Greek myth, after Jason, leader of the Argonauts, stole the Golden Fleece, he had to fight an army of soldiers that had sprouted from dragon's teeth sown in the ground by the witch Medea (*above*). The Greek goddess of magic, Hecate (*right*), was widely feared. Each month, offerings were placed at crossroads as a sacrifice, including lambs, garlic, cheese – and black puppies!

SMELLS A BIT FISHY?

Many tales also use ancient magical symbols. For example, the symbol of a fish with a golden key (*left*) stands for a new member of a magic group swimming between the real and spiritual worlds and swallowing a key that will unlock the wisdom of both worlds.

The three women cackled as they tossed the ingredients into the pot: eye of toad; spider's legs; sweat of camel's armpit; and the little black bits you get between your toes when you don't bathe...

The cauldron fizzed with a bright green light as it was stirred. "I hope they put on their outfits," said Nathan. "I bet they wear black pointed hats."

Miss Proctor's nose wrinkled as she took a sip. "Mmm — I love the way the spider's legs always get caught in my teeth!" She dipped her mug into the pot, and, with a twinkle in her eye, drank deeply...

Rachel stifled a scream as she looked on in horror. The room filled with the sound of cracking bones as the old woman began to writhe uncontrollably. Emily felt quite ill when a bright yellow puss began to seep from the boils on the witch's face. Then, as suddenly as it had started, it was over. Old Miss Proctor was now a sprightly 25-year-old! "I knew I'd put in too much baboon's tongue," she laughed.

In medieval times, most Europeans believed in magic. Many villages had "wise women" and "wise men." They made herbal potions to bring good luck and looked into the future by examining kitchen tools, like shears. In fact, the English word *witch* comes from the Anglo-Saxon word *wicca*, which meant wise one.

SHOW ME A MIRACLE!

Even after the arrival of Christianity, many of the old pagan religions survived, such as the Celtic worship of magical gods like the "Green Man" (*left*).

Early Christianity itself is full of magical stories and superstitions. For example, Saint Patrick was supposed to have rid Ireland of all snakes. And even as late as the 13th-century, the Christian Abbess Hildegarde recommended wearing a belt made of deerskin to ward off evil spirits.

THE RISE OF THE "EVIL" WITCHES

By the 15th century, the Church had decided that magic and superstition were the devil's work, and that witches were evil (*left*).

This change in view can be seen in the medieval story of Rapunzel, where a witch uses her magic to help a couple have a baby daughter. The wicked witch then takes the child Rapunzel, imprisons her in a tower, and visits her by climbing up the girl's long hair (*above right*). Tales like this showed people that witches could no longer be trusted.

CRASH! The bucket that Rachel was standing on toppled over. With a scream, she fell to the ground. Miss Proctor rushed to the window, and Nathan froze as he gazed into her fiery eyes.

"Run for it," shouted Emily. Rachel scrambled to her feet, and raced after the other two. With hearts pounding, the children ran down the nearest alley. "Quick, let's take a short cut through the cemetery," Nathan panted as he waited for Rachel.

The sight of Miss Proctor struck terror into their hearts. She glided towards them, her hair writhing like snakes, her face twisted into a silent scream of rage. Nathan rushed into the cemetery, but caught his foot on an old tombstone and fell. Soon he felt the foul breath of the witch upon his face — there was no escape...

WITCH HUNT!

In 1486, Heinrich Kraemer and Jakob Sprenger, two German priests, produced a witch-hunter's handbook, known as *The Witches' Hammer*.

Pope Innocent VIII gave the book his blessing and soon professional witch hunters sprang up all over Europe. Over the next 150 years, nearly 300,000 "witches" were executed.

A MEETING WITH THE DEVIL

Witches often confessed to taking part in Sabbats (*above*) – drunken feasts and rituals with the devil. But such confessions were usually given under torture and there is little evidence that Sabbats took place. In England, in 1584, Reginald Scott wrote that most witches were simply old people

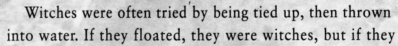

unable to answer back, but the executions continued.

Witches were often tried by being tied up, then thrown into water. If they floated, they were witches, but if they drowned, they were innocent! The guilty were burned at the stake (*left* and *above right*).

THE SALEM WITCH TRIALS

In Salem, Massachusetts, in 1692, a group of girls were thought to be bewitched (affected by witchcraft). At a trial they accused people of putting spells on them and 21 people and two dogs were executed as witches. This event was made into a powerful play, *The Crucible*, by Arthur Miller (filmed in 1996, *right*).

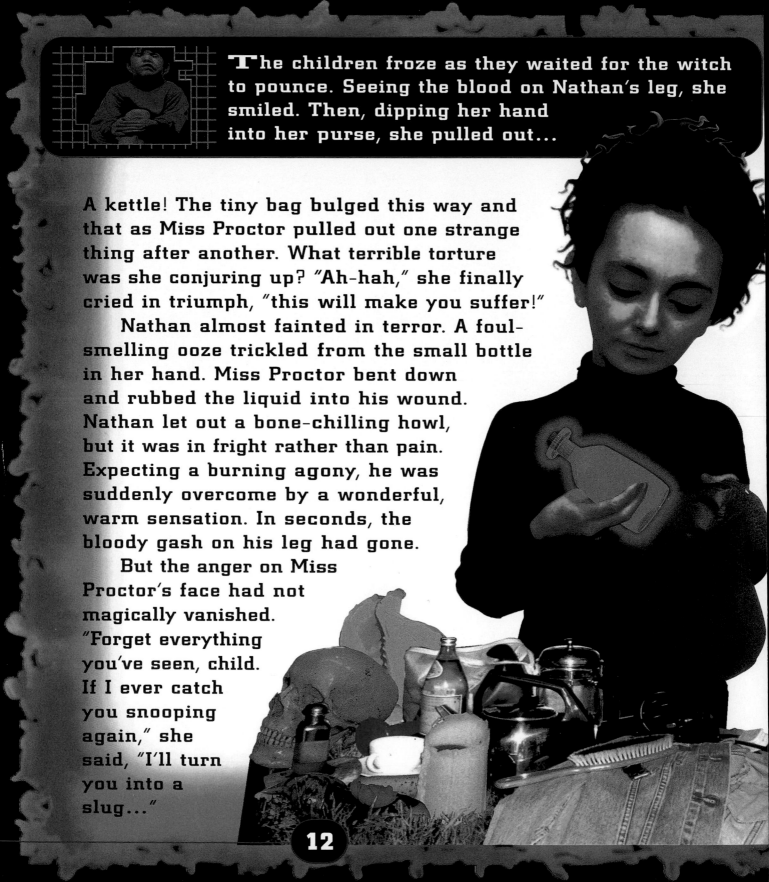

The children froze as they waited for the witch to pounce. Seeing the blood on Nathan's leg, she smiled. Then, dipping her hand into her purse, she pulled out...

A kettle! The tiny bag bulged this way and that as Miss Proctor pulled out one strange thing after another. What terrible torture was she conjuring up? "Ah-hah," she finally cried in triumph, "this will make you suffer!"

Nathan almost fainted in terror. A foul-smelling ooze trickled from the small bottle in her hand. Miss Proctor bent down and rubbed the liquid into his wound. Nathan let out a bone-chilling howl, but it was in fright rather than pain. Expecting a burning agony, he was suddenly overcome by a wonderful, warm sensation. In seconds, the bloody gash on his leg had gone.

But the anger on Miss Proctor's face had not magically vanished. "Forget everything you've seen, child. If I ever catch you snooping again," she said, "I'll turn you into a slug..."

WITCHES' POWERS

Many people's first images of witches are women flying on broomsticks (*right*), changing from old hags into beautiful young women, or gazing deeply into a crystal ball. But could they really do these things?

FLYING TONIGHT

A belief in a witch's ability to fly has been around since before the time of the *The Golden Ass*, a story by Greek writer Apuleius (c. A.D. 125-170). In this, the witch Pamphile turns herself into an owl by smearing herself with a magic ointment. Ancient spells for flying all contained strong drugs that caused an impression of falling through the air, so maybe the witches just thought they were flying!

"Glamour" was originally the power to hypnotize people into seeing illusion as reality. So, as in our story, older women could magically appear young again – a trick that is performed with makeup on a daily basis today!

LOOKING INTO THE FUTURE

Divination, or obtaining knowledge of future events by "magical" means, is an ancient practice using a variety of methods. Three of the most common are palmistry (reading people's hands), gazing into crystal balls (*above*), and reading tarot cards (*right*). In the past, divination offered people a way to ease strain and worry – fortune-tellers earn less if they only have bad news to tell! It also offered people faced with a difficult decision a ready-made answer.

That night, Nathan thought about Miss Proctor. If witches were so bad, then why had she healed his wound? Early next morning, he sneaked around to Rachel and Emily's house.

Soon all three were heading back to the witch's house. This time, Nathan was armed with a huge bunch of flowers. Nervously, he lifted the huge brass knocker. But before he had time to bring it down, the door swung open. Emily let out a little scream. An eerie voice spoke from inside. "If you think you'll win me over with a few flowers — you must know me better than I thought."

Two mugs of cocoa later, Sophie Proctor had told them her story — how she was the guardian of an ancient spell book that showed the site of the Stone of Fate; how the stone gave incredible powers to the person who unlocked its secret; and how a powerful wizard, banished for practicing the forbidden arts, had come in disguise to their town in search of the stone. But who was this evil sorcerer?

When Christian Crusaders traveled to the Holy Land in the 11th century, they came into contact with the magical traditions of the East (*left*). They brought back the *Picatrix*, an Arab handbook of practical (or "natural") magic, which became popular in later medieval Europe.

ABRACADABRA
BRACADABR
RACADAB
ACADA
CAD
A

INDESTRUCTIBLE GRIMOIRES

From the 16th century, the old spells began to be written down again, in books called grimoires (*right*). These contained details about fortune-telling, summoning evil spirits, poisonous brews, and becoming invisible. Some explained how the charm word *Abracadabra* (*above right*) could cure illness. As the word grew smaller, so your fever was supposed to fade away.

According to legend, you could burn, bury, or throw grimoires into the sea, but the next day they would appear again on your bookshelf!

THE POWER OF NUMBERS

The mystic power of numbers was an important part of the Eastern tradition. For example, the number 5 was a charm against the evil eye (*see* page 31). Magic squares were used to represent the numbers of demons associated with each of the planets. The numbers in each vertical and horizontal line add up to the same number, the magical number of the planet's demon. This magic square (*left*) represents the planet Mars.

Over the next few weeks, the four of them became good friends. And now that Sophie looked so young, she was introduced to everyone as Miss Proctor's niece!

One day, as they sat watching her cat Greediguts chasing a bird around the garden, Sophie suddenly jumped up. "Fiddlesticks," she cried, "after 400 years it's about time I passed on some of my skills. Let's do some magic!"

With a snap of her fingers, Sophie showed them why her house was always so clean! Mops, brooms, and cleaners flew about the house, sweeping and washing every nook and cranny. Then the children had a go. Rachel soon had flowers sprouting from Nathan's ears and Emily managed to float in the air.

But when Nathan tried to make a rabbit bark like a dog, it all went horribly wrong. He got the magic words mixed up, and Sophie had to act quickly to stop the mad wailing voices he had summoned from tearing his head apart...

SPELLS AND POTIONS

Some of the ingredients in the grimoires' spells sound like a fail-safe recipe for being sick. Common choices were (*right*, in clockwise order) mistletoe, mandrake root, snake, toad, and deadly nightshade. Others seem to be chosen for their power to make the recipe-taster drunk.

MAGIC PLANTS

A great variety of plants used to be collected for their powers to heal and protect from evil spirits – some still are. People believed that plants even resembled the parts they were supposed to cure. For example, the shiny onion was used for head complaints, especially baldness! Strong-smelling plants, such as garlic, were best for keeping away spirits.

The Greek philosopher Pythagoras (born 580 B.C.) believed that sweet-smelling flowers contained the souls of the dead. In legend, he was killed after being chased into a field of flowers by enemy soldiers. Not wanting to step on the dead, he was soon caught!

KISSING UNDER THE MISTLETOE

The tradition of kissing under the mistletoe dates back to the time when Christmas was a pagan festival worshiped by Celtic priests, called Druids (*left*). Mistletoe was known by the Druids as the "all-healer," a view shared by the Ainus of Japan.

Nathan's failed spell showed what a dangerous thing magic could be. Deep down, Miss Proctor knew it was only a matter of time before one of the children was tempted by the dark side.

For weeks, Tracy Turnbull had teased the twins. "That Miss Proctor's niece," she squawked, "she's such a weirdo." Emily's eyes flashed with anger. "As you behave like such a pig," she spat out, "maybe you should be one."

Before Rachel or Nathan could stop her, Emily spoke the magic words, "toxus, flexa, mixtus porcus." Tracy tried to scream — but all that came out was a squeal. Her ears stretched into points, sprouting stiff white hairs, and her nose wrinkled into an ugly snout.

"Quick," shouted Rachel, "let's get her out of here before anyone sees." But it was too late. A dark figure grinned in the shadows. These children would surely lead him to the sacred spell book.

Magical rituals live on in ways that you may not realize. In fact, many of today's festivals and superstitions were originally linked to witches and witchcraft.

MAGICAL FESTIVALS

The Celtic festival of Samhain is probably the source of today's Halloween (*left*). The Druids, the priests of the Celts, built huge bonfires and sacrificed animals, crops, and possibly humans on them. In Christian times, Halloween became the night when witches gathered to meet the devil. People in England carved out beets and potatoes and put candles inside to use as lanterns to frighten the witches away. When the custom reached America, beets and potatoes were replaced by pumpkins.

SUPERSTITIONS

Many old superstitions still live on, helping people overcome their fears by providing security. For example, finding a horseshoe (*left*) or a four-leaf clover (*top right*) is said to bring good luck. The tradition of sailors having tattoos (*above right*) dates back to the belief that these decorations would protect them from being whipped as punishment. Others include plucking the petals off a flower to find out the feelings of a loved one (*right*).

Sophie frowned as she looked the poor girl up and down. "What did she do to deserve this?" she scolded Emily. "I'm very disappointed in you. Magic is a gift — you must use it wisely."

While Emily sulked in the corner, Sophie wove a spell around the sobbing child. The pig's ears and nose melted away to be replaced by the girl's natural features. Then Sophie uttered some strange, dark words, and seconds later, Tracy Turnbull had forgotten everything.

Emily stomped down the road, angry at Sophie's words. Suddenly, a dark figure appeared from nowhere. "Hello, child. I see you've had enough of Sophie Proctor's silly spells. How would you like to learn some *real* magic? Just steal Miss Proctor's spell book for me." Emily couldn't wait to have her revenge, and nodded in agreement.

That night, mad laughter could be heard coming from the chemistry labs. "Soon, all will be mine!" a voice cried in triumph.

MAGICAL SCIENCE

Until the early 18th century, there was little to separate science and magic in many people's minds. But this was a world before the scientific revolution of the last 300 years. Many of today's scientists (*bottom*), working on miracle drugs, ways to prolong life, robots, and journeys to Mars have the same aims as alchemists (magical scientists), and would have been accused of witchcraft!

THE SECRET OF ETERNAL LIFE

The two main aims of alchemy were to discover the elixir (secret) of life, a potion that allowed people to live forever, and to find a way of turning cheap metals into gold.

To help with their investigation, alchemists (*above right*) were supposed to be pure in heart and mind. They wrote down their experiments using special symbols (*left*), just as scientists today use letters for elements.

MATH AND MAGIC

Famous medieval alchemists included Roger Bacon (1214–1292), the inventor of gunpowder in Europe, and Albertus Magnus (1193–1280), a bishop who carried out many real experiments but was said to be a magician. In one tale, he brought a robot to life, but destroyed it because it talked too much!

Even the brilliant mathematician Sir Isaac Newton (1642–1727), more famous for his important theories on gravity and the universe, spent many of his later years studying alchemy.

"**C**an I have another cookie?" Emily smiled sweetly at Sophie. Secretly, her mind was on other things. Where did Miss Proctor keep the sacred spell book, and how was she going to get it?

Her chance came just hours later. Not only did Sophie show the grimoire to Rachel, watched by Emily through a hole in the study door, but she even suggested going out for a walk to collect plants for a potion. Emily said she felt sleepy, then walked toward home until the others were out of sight. Then, running around to the back of Miss Proctor's house, where she had left a kitchen window open, she wriggled inside and walked swiftly to the study.

Emily stood on tiptoe next to the bookshelf, stretching a hand up to where she had seen Sophie hide the spell book. Her fingers skimmed along the dusty shelf, searching desperately for the spell book's rough crocodile-skin cover. Was that it..."AAARGH!"

Emily screamed in agony as Greediguts sank his teeth into her leg and slashed at her with his claws. Feeling the scaly cover at last, she grabbed the book and ran from the hissing cat.

ANIMAL MAGIC

Many animals have been linked to sorcery. For example, witches were thought to borrow horses (*bottom left*) at night and take them on rides through the darkness. So, next time you see gleaming horse brasses, remember that these were made to ward off witches looking for a free ride!

A FAMILIAR STORY

The "familiar" was a demon in animal form that helped a witch with her magic, feeding on spoonfuls of her blood (*above right*). Most familiars were small animals, like cats, toads, or moles (*left*), and were given names by their owners like Hiff Hiff, Greediguts, and Pyewacket.

The belief in familiars made it very easy for witch-hunters, who got paid for each conviction. Old people living alone have always enjoyed pets for company, and could be accused of having a familiar.

WHAT A CAT-ASTROPHE

How do animals become linked to good or bad magic? Take the cat, which even today is thought to bring bad luck in some countries. It started off as the kindly Egyptian goddess, Bastet (*right*). Then Celtic cat goddesses, such as the Blue Hag of Scotland and Black Annis, demanded human sacrifice.

By medieval times, the cat was the number one familiar in trials, and thousands were burned at the stake with their owners. Maybe its fierce independence, eerie cries at night, and eyes that appear to glow in the dark also made it look sinister.

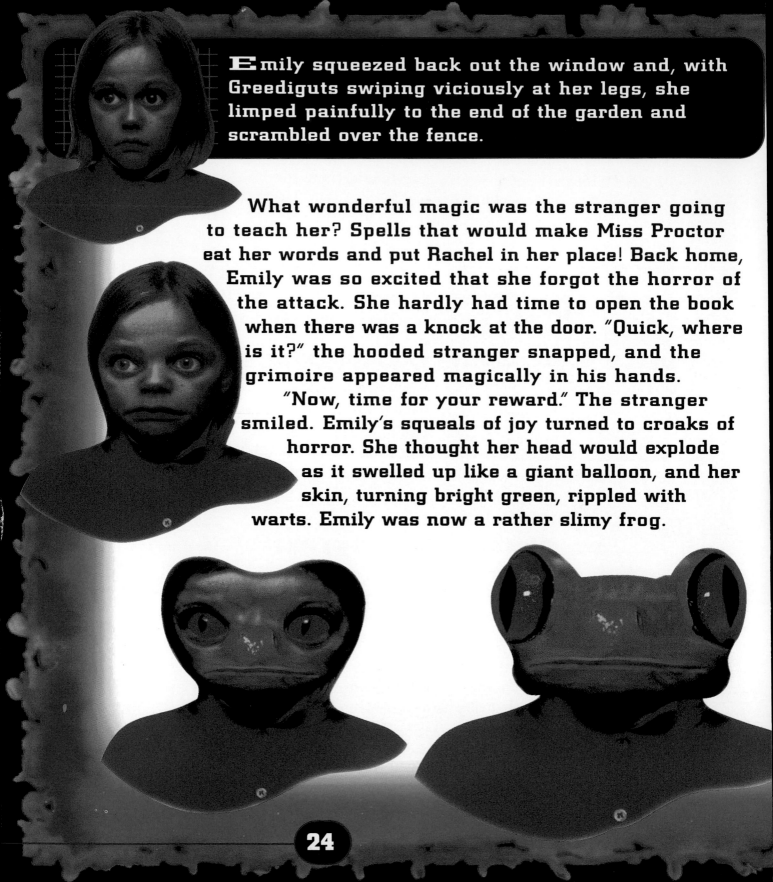

Emily squeezed back out the window and, with Greediguts swiping viciously at her legs, she limped painfully to the end of the garden and scrambled over the fence.

What wonderful magic was the stranger going to teach her? Spells that would make Miss Proctor eat her words and put Rachel in her place! Back home, Emily was so excited that she forgot the horror of the attack. She hardly had time to open the book when there was a knock at the door. "Quick, where is it?" the hooded stranger snapped, and the grimoire appeared magically in his hands.

"Now, time for your reward." The stranger smiled. Emily's squeals of joy turned to croaks of horror. She thought her head would explode as it swelled up like a giant balloon, and her skin, turning bright green, rippled with warts. Emily was now a rather slimy frog.

WITCH DOCTORS

Sorcery is not just a feature of European culture. In Africa, witches are said to be possessed by evil spirits. To "cure" them, witch doctors, or "witch smellers" as they are sometimes known, track down the spirits and cast them out of the witch's body. They can also trap spirits in statues (*right*) to protect the owner against bad magic or the "evil eye."

HERBAL HEALERS

Most witch doctors are also experts at preparing herbal cures (*left*). They are still popular partly because many African people simply cannot afford modern medicines. In 1976, the World Health Organization recommended that witch doctors should join their medical teams, and medical doctors are recognizing that many of their cures have a sound scientific foundation.

MAGIC IN THE FAMILY?

Traditionally, African magic was divided into witchcraft and sorcery. Witches were usually women who had inherited their magical powers. They were said to grow fat on the flesh of their victims, and their familiars were hyenas, owls, and baboons (*bottom left*).

According to tradition, sorcery could be learned by anyone, and involved spells that, like European superstitions, helped to bring good or bad luck. Powerful potions might transform a person into a leopard (*right*).

At that moment, on the other side of town, Rachel felt a shiver down her spine. "Did you feel that, too?" asked Sophie. "I have a feeling that something terrible has happened to Emily."

They rushed back to the house, dropping some of the herbs they had collected in their hurry to get back. As they came closer, Greediguts shot out through the gate. "What's up, old friend?," said Miss Proctor, dizzy with trying to focus on the cat as it scampered around and around.

In frustration, she grabbed the cat, carried it inside, and placed it on the table. Then, closing her eyes, she waved her hands in the air in strange, mystical patterns. From her fingers came a swirling mist that bathed the cat in a bright glow. To Nathan and Rachel's amazement, Greediguts started talking in a deep voice.

"Miss Proctor," it explained, "young Emily has been tempted by the forces of evil. She came for the grimoire, summoned by the one whom we must fear. Punish me, for I could not stop her from taking it." So the spell book had gone — but who had Emily given it to?

EASTERN SORCERY

The power of the supernatural still runs deep in Eastern culture. Many Chinese people believe strongly in *feng shui*, the power of "wind and water" to bring good or bad luck to buildings. Special mirrors (*left*) are often used to ward off evil spirits.

CALLING UP SPIRITS

Muslims believed in *Jinn*, or genie, spirits made of fire that could be tamed with the words, *Azamtu atalkum*, "I command you." Sorcerers were said to conjure up these spirits, sometimes in animal form,

like this creature from the movie *The Golden Voyage of Sinbad*, 1973 (*above*). Perhaps the most famous *Jinn* is the one that appears in the story of Aladdin.

CHINESE ALCHEMY

Chinese myth and legend is full of magic (this scary sorcerer appears in the 1989 movie, *Big Trouble in Little China*, *left*). Like European alchemists, Chinese doctors searched for the "elixir of life," which they believed was made of liquid gold, a metal that never loses its shine.

Sun Ssu-miao, a Chinese alchemist, wrote *Great Secrets of Alchemy* in the 7th century A.D. Its recipes contain such poisonous substances as arsenic and mercury, certain to cause a stomach ache! A tastier part of the Chinese magical tradition survives today – the practice of eating fortune cookies – each with a delightful prediction inside (*above right*).

Sophie paced up and down the room, twisting a lock of hair tighter and tighter around her fingers as she concentrated on how to track down Emily and retrieve the stolen spell book.

All of a sudden, she stopped dead. Of course — why not use Rachel! By following the magical thread that exists between twins, she could find where Emily was. Hurriedly, Sophie shut the blinds, lit a candle, and turned off the lights.

She stuck her finger and thumb in her left ear, and pulled out the fattest worm Nathan had ever seen. Without hesitating, she bit its head off and ground the worm into a paste.

Rachel wasn't too eager to taste the potion, but it became easier when Miss Proctor transformed it into a bar of chocolate. With just one nibble, an eerie glow lit the darkened room and the image of a man laughing over a frog filled Rachel's eyes. Nathan stared in disbelief. "It's Mr. Raven, my science teacher..."

SHAMANS AND SPIRITS

To most Native American peoples, magic was a part of religion. They believed a great mystical force controlled the world, and good and bad spirits linked humans with this force. It was the role of the medicine man, or shaman, to protect them from the bad spirits.

SPIRIT CENTERS

One of the most visible signs of these beliefs is "Big Medicine Wheel," a series of stone circles used for shamanistic rituals in Arizona (*above*). Equally famous are the beautiful totem poles carved by the Algonquin peoples in the northwestern part of North America (*right*). A totem, meaning "guardian spirit" in Algonquin, is a sacred object that protects a tribe against bad spirits. Totems can be plants, animals, or objects.

HEALING POWERS

Among the Ojibway tribe in Canada, shamans called *jossakid* fought spirits in a "shaking tent," while others called *wabeno* practiced fire magic. But the shaman also had a medical role. Holding magic charms and chanting special phrases, the shaman (*bottom left*) hoped to "suck" evil spirits out of the victim's body. Today's shamans, like Rolling Thunder (*above left*), are being asked to show their skills to doctors.

Rachel and Nathan ran helter-skelter as they collected ingredients for the spells that Miss Proctor planned to use on Mr. Raven. With such a powerful wizard, she had to take every precaution.

"Rachel, come with me," said Sophie, "since I need you to find Emily. But I think it best if you stay behind, Nathan." But when she saw the look on his face, she knew he would follow anyway. "OK. Come if you must, but this is no game. Both of you, drink some of this potion of invisibility."

Miss Proctor threw open the door to the garden, and taking their hands, cried out to the moon. "Hecate, invest in me your wings of flight, that I may travel through the night." She rose into the sky, gently pulling the two children with her. As they swooped above the rooftops, their clothes flapped wildly in the breeze.

PROTECTION

What could people do to protect themselves from witches? Some used special plants, such as rue, vervain, and dill. In the East, there was a constant fear of the "evil eye." This belief stemmed from the idea that the glance of certain people can bring disaster and ruin. As protection, people wore fish charms, chains of glass eyes, or red coral necklaces. In Greece, it was enough just to spit or say the word "garlic!"

GATES, POSTS, AND BOTTLES

In European folklore, the best way to defeat a witch was to use a witch bottle (*left*). Those fearing a witch filled the bottle with their own urine, some hair, nail clippings, and any sharp objects, such as nails or thorns. The bottle was then corked and boiled at midnight, to torment the witch. If the bottle burst, the witch died, but if the cork flew out, she escaped!

Many English churches have a gate at their boundary wall (*right*) – this was originally designed to keep witches at bay. Some English houses are protected by "witch posts," oak pillars with a crooked sixpence tucked into a hole in their center.

THE SIN-EATER

One way of preventing evil spirits was "sin-eating." A person was paid to take the sins of a dead person so they were free to go to heaven. To do this, the sin-eater placed dishes of salt and bread on the chest of the corpse, and ate them (*left*).

Mr. Raven couldn't believe his luck. It had been so simple. One foolish child's greed, and here he was, face to face with the Stone of Fate, just minutes away from awesome power.

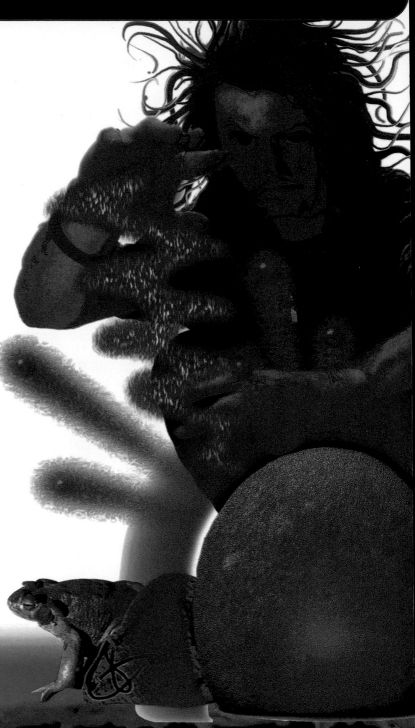

The bag in his hand wriggled, and the wizard chuckled as he pulled out the frog that had once been Emily. It's unfortunate the spell didn't require him to sacrifice this ugly creature.

Instead, placing the frog on the stone, he tied a ribbon around its belly, and sprinkled a few drops of bat blood over its back. Then, reading from the spell book, he began to chant magic words.

The Stone of Fate vibrated in the ground, sending ripples of energy across the valley. Almost there, he thought, when WHOOOSH, a falcon swooped down from the sky, grabbing the frog from the stone and breaking the spell. Mr. Raven howled in rage. Whoever had dared to spoil his plans must die!

WITCHES IN FICTION

The world's fairy tales are packed with magic and sorcery, from the wicked witch in *Snow White* (*right*) to the evil enchantress in *Sleeping Beauty*. One of the most terrifying witches is the Russian, Baba Yaga. She is a repulsive old hag, and her teeth, nose, and breasts are made of iron. The house she lives in is surrounded by a fence made from the bones of people she has eaten, and she flies around the countryside in a giant pestle (*left*).

SELLING YOUR SOUL TO THE DEVIL

Many great plays also have magic as a theme. In the legend of *Doctor Faustus,* a bored scientist turns to magic. He summons up a servant of darkness and sells his soul to the devil (*bottom right*). In return, he can have whatever he wants for 24 years!

Magic appears in several plays by William Shakespeare (1564–1616). In *Macbeth* (1606), the main character meets three witches who predict that he will become King of Scotland (*left*).

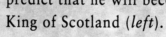

WITCH POEMS

In his poem *The Sorcerer's Apprentice* (made into a cartoon by Walt Disney), German Johann von Goethe (1749–1832) described a young helper who is overwhelmed by the magical powers he has summoned. In *The Witch of Atlas,* English poet Percy Shelley (1792–1822) tried to change popular views of sorcery by describing a beautiful witch who uses her magic for good.

Mr. Raven turned into a giant eagle with long, sharp talons that glinted in the moonlight. With a few beats of his powerful wings the eagle was aloft, seeking out the falcon with his flashing red eyes.

Already the falcon had changed back into human form. It was that meddling witch Sophie Proctor — he should have known!

Back on the ground, Sophie had hardly finished picking off the last of the falcon skin when she saw the eagle screaming toward her. Think fast, think fast. There, in the grass, she saw a slithering shape. In the blink of an eye, Sophie turned herself into a huge, writhing serpent. With lightning speed, the snake struck, and wrapped its massive coils around the eagle. But as its grip tightened, the bird evaporated into mist.

From the vapor emerged a monstrous bear-like creature with slavering jaws. Nathan and Rachel could only watch in frozen horror as it sprang at Sophie. Faced with such a beast, her magic was useless.

MOVIE WITCHES

Though most people today do not believe in witches, they remain a popular subject in movies for both children and adults.

COMPLETELY WIZARD

Many witch movies depict the eternal struggle between good and evil magic, as in the 1978 cartoon adaptation of J.R.R.

Tolkien's classic story *Lord of the Rings (below right)*. The 1981 movie *Excalibur (above left)*, based on the medieval tales of King Arthur, focused on the battle between the wizard Merlin and the sorceress Morgan Le Fay, Arthur's half-sister.

In the 1939 movie, *The Wizard of Oz (below left)*, the heroine Dorothy is helped by the good witch of the South against the wicked witch of the West.

A SCHOOL FOR WITCHES?

Some scary movies have also been made about witches living in the modern world. In *The Craft* (1996, *below right*), three high school girls try to bully a former member of their secret coven

by sending plagues of insects and worms into her home, but she defeats them by using magical powers inherited from her mother.

In the 1987 movie *The Witches of Eastwick*, three witches, bored by life in a sleepy New England town, conjure up the perfect man to keep them company. However, things get nasty when he turns out to be the devil!

Miss Proctor, dazed by the crushing weight of the bear monster, lay still and helpless as Mr. Raven roughly tied her hands and feet with rope.

"Just sit back and watch," he taunted. Meanwhile, Emily the frog hopped bravely away. "Enough playing games," Mr. Raven thought as he began stomping on the ground in an effort to crush her with his boots. How long could the frog avoid him?

Long enough for Nathan and Rachel to sneak up to Sophie and start untying the cords that bound her. But their invisibility was wearing off — fast. Mr. Raven saw two pairs of legs kneeling behind Sophie. Leaving the frog again, he raced over and grabbed their still invisible heads.

Nathan and Rachel screamed — but they had done enough. Now free of her ropes, Miss Proctor called on the power of her sister witches and summoned up a storm. Thunder roared and lightning flashed, and a whirlwind swept from her hands, picking up the wizard and smashing him against a tree.

As we have seen already, there have been real and imaginary witches across the world for thousands of years. But are there any still around?

TRICK OF THE EYE

This faded photograph (*left*) shows a French witch, Näia, from the early part of the 20th century, giving a consultation. In contrast, some modern witches, like David Copperfield (*right*), are illusionists who use props and tricks of the eye to fool their audience (*top right*).

THE GENTLE SPELL MAKERS

Since the fall of Russian communism in 1989, *kolduns*, or witches, returned to the mainstream of Russian life. They have even appeared on television! They claim they can use good magic to perform a

variety of tasks for their clients, such as finding stolen cars and arranging love matches. Some charge thousands of dollars, but the traditional healing witches (*left*) work for bags of food from poor clients.

Most people claiming to be witches in Europe and the United States today are more interested in traditional medicine than in summoning demons or casting horrible spells on people. Modern druids (*right*), for example, stress the importance of living in harmony with nature rather than human sacrifice!

Sophie Proctor, still shaking from the effort of that final spell, placed her hands on the Stone of Fate. "For thousands of years, witches have sought this stone for the power it brings them, but now that I've seen it, I'm terrified of what it might do in the wrong hands. However, I must use its power to rid the world of this evil wizard."

At her touch the stone hummed again, and little streaks of colored light danced about her face and hair. Then she walked across to the wizard, and placing her hands on his shoulders, kissed him on the forehead. The wizard's eyes blinked open, and Rachel screamed.

"Hush, there is nothing to fear," said Sophie. "Mr. Raven will never again feel the force of magic pulsing through his veins. And if he knows what's good for him, he'll keep well away from here."

Just then, a dazed and confused Emily emerged from the trees. She was still removing the remains of the frog's skin from her face. "I hope you've learned your lesson," said Sophie. Emily looked down at the ground, her face a picture of shame. But she would remember this place, and the powers of the Stone of Fate. She would be back.

WITCHES' WORDS

Alchemy The "magical" science that searched for a substance that brings eternal life and also for the means of turning base metals into gold.

Amulet A magical charm, carried by a person to ward off evil.

Astrology The belief that lives and personalities are influenced by the planets and stars.

Cauldron A large cooking pot often used by witches for making potions.

Charm Words or objects supposed to protect from spells.

Devil's marks Marks on the body, such as scars or warts, that have been put there by the devil to identify his followers.

Divination Ways of looking into the future, e.g. gazing at crystal balls.

Druids Celtic sorcerers from the Bronze Age. Modern druids perform pagan rituals rather than magic.

Familiar A creature, such as a cat, a toad, or a baboon, that helps a witch perform her magic.

Glamour The power to hypnotize people into seeing illusion as reality.

Grimoire A spell book.

Horoscope A chart of astrological predictions.

Jinn A Muslim spirit made from fire.

Metamorphosis Transformation from one type of body to another; for example, a witch might metamorphose into a cat.

Numerology Fortune-telling by using significant numbers.

Palmistry Fortune-telling by the study of hands.

Ritual A formal religious or magical ceremony.

Sabbat A gathering of witches.

Shaman A magician-priest from the peoples of North America and Siberia, who formed a link with the spirit world.

Spell Words or movements that make magic happen.

Totem A Native American word for an object that represented the spirit of a person or group.

Wizard A male witch, or warlock.

INDEX

PHOTOCREDITS
Abbreviations: t – top, m – middle, b – bottom, r – right, l – left.
Pages 5t, 13b, 17m, 23tr, 33t & br & 37tl – Mary Evans Picture Library. 5m, 9m, 11ml, 13tr, 25t & m, 29t & bl & 39 – Fortean Picture Library. 5b, 13mr, 17b, 19mr, 25b, 29br, 37tr, m & b – Frank Spooner Pictures. 7t, 7br, 9b, 11t, 15, 21t, 23b & 33bl – AKG London. 11t – Neue Constantin ZDF (courtesy Kobal). 13ml – Warner Brothers (courtesy Kobal). 21t – Glaxo Holdings. 27t & 35b – Columbia Pictures (courtesy Kobal). 27bl – 20th Centruy Fox (courtesy Kobal). 35t – Orion/Warner Brothers (courtesy Kobal). 35mr – MGM (courtesy Kobal). 11b & 35ml – Kobal Collection.

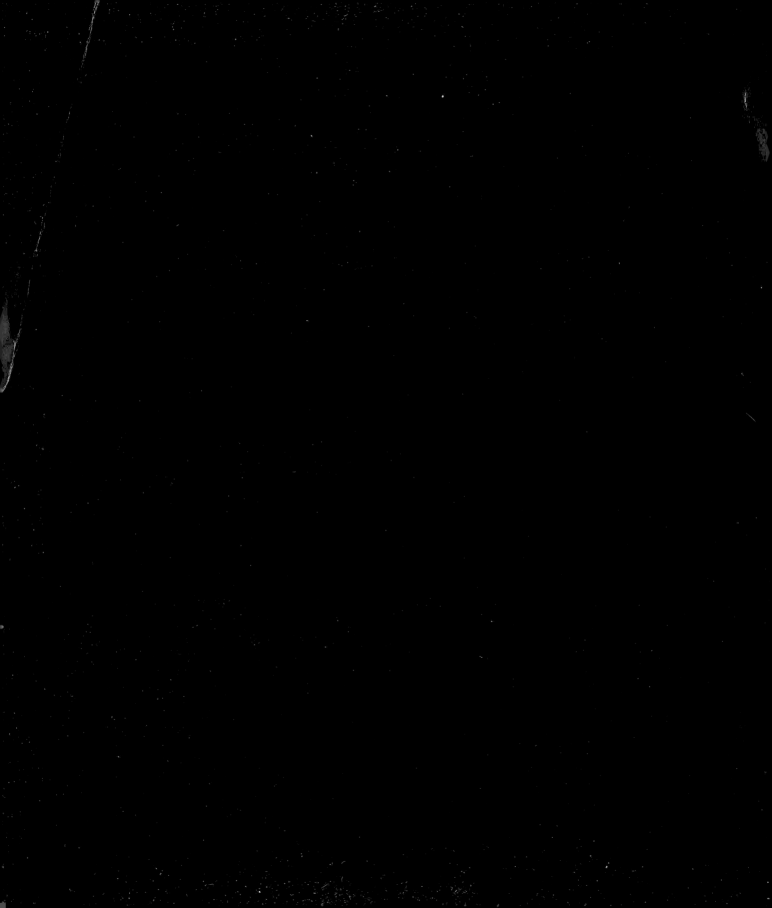